ALEX
KUSKOWSKI

A FUN AND CREATIVE INTRODUCTION TO FIBER ART

COOL

SEWING

for KIDS

Checkerboard
Library

An Imprint of Abdo Publishing
www.abdopublishing.com

VISIT US AT WWW.ABDOPUBLISHING.COM

Published by Abdo Publishing, a division of ABDO, PO Box 398166, Minneapolis, Minnesota 55439. Copyright © 2015 by Abdo Consulting Group, Inc. International copyrights reserved in all countries. No part of this book may be reproduced in any form without written permission from the publisher. Checkerboard Library™ is a trademark and logo of Abdo Publishing.

Printed in the United States of America, North Mankato, Minnesota
062014
092014

THIS BOOK CONTAINS RECYCLED MATERIALS

Design and Production: Anders Hanson, Mighty Media, Inc.
Series Editor: Liz Salzmann
Photo Credits: Anders Hanson, Shutterstock

The following manufacturers/names appearing in this book are trademarks: New York Color®

Library of Congress Cataloging-in-Publication Data
Kuskowski, Alex., author.
  Cool sewing for kids : a fun and creative introduction to fiber art / Alex Kuskowski.
     pages cm. -- (Cool fiber art)
  Audience: Ages 8-10.
  Includes bibliographical references and index.
  ISBN 978-1-62403-311-7 (alk. paper)
  1. Sewing--Juvenile literature. I. Title.
  TT712.K87 2015
  746--dc23
                        2013043076

TO ADULT HELPERS

This is your chance to assist someone new to crafting! As children learn to craft they develop new skills, gain confidence, and make cool things. These activities are designed to help children learn how to make their own craft projects. Some activities may need more assistance than others. Be there to offer guidance when they need it. Encourage them to do as much as they can on their own. Be a cheerleader for their creativity.

Before getting started, remember to lay down ground rules for using the crafting tools and cleaning up. There should always be adult supervision when a child uses a sharp tool.

TABLE OF CONTENTS

Sew Cool

Discover the world of sewing! Sewing is attaching pieces of fabric together using a needle and thread. People have been sewing since the Stone Age.

Sewing is one of the most useful crafts! You can use sewing to fix clothes. Or you can use it to make fun new things.

All you need to start are fabric, needles, and thread. This book will give you an **overview** of basic steps, terms, and **patterns**. Step-by-step instructions make learning a breeze. You'll love to show off the things you make. Just turn the page and get into sewing.

Tools of the Trade

NEEDLES

Needles come in different sizes. The higher the number, the smaller the needle. Embroidery needles are numbered 1 though 12. **Chenille** and **tapestry** needles are numbered 18 through 26.

Embroidery needles

Chenille needles

FABRIC

You can sew any fabric. Some **patterns** suggest using a certain kind of fabric.

Almost all fabric has two sides, the front and back. The color or pattern on the front is brighter. The duller side is the back.

THREAD

There are many different kinds of thread. The projects in this book use sewing thread and embroidery floss. Sewing thread has one strand. Embroidery floss has six strands twisted together. You sometimes need to separate the strands and only use some of them.

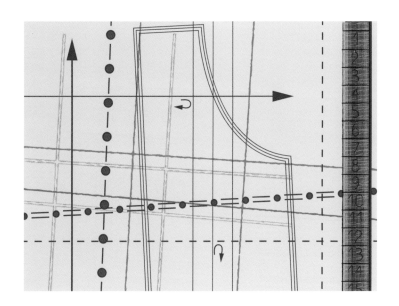

PATTERNS

Sewing **patterns** come with directions. They list the types of needles, thread, and fabric needed for the project. There are tons of fun patterns to choose from!

PINS

Pins keep the fabric in place while you sew. They are especially helpful when sewing curved or **complicated** shapes. But be careful! They are sharp.

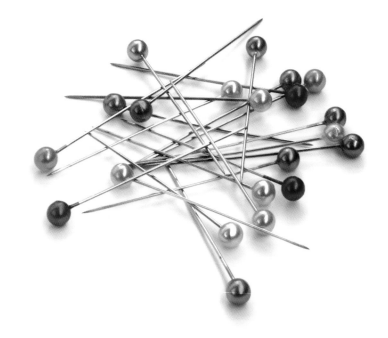

It's In the Bag

Keep a bag to hold your pins, fabric, patterns, and general craft supplies like the ones below!

BAG

BEADS AND BUTTONS

MEASURING TAPE

PEN AND PAPER

NEEDLES

SCISSORS

GLUE

SAFETY PINS

THREAD

⁂ Basics ⁂

NEEDLE NOSE

How to thread a needle.

Cut a piece of thread 20 inches (51 cm) long. Tie a knot 3 inches (7.5 cm) from one end. Thread the other end through the needle. Pull it through 5 inches (13 cm).

MAKE YOUR FIRST STITCH

This is the basis for every stitch!

Push the needle through the fabric from back to front. Pull until the knot hits the back of the fabric.

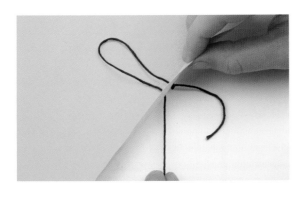

Push the needle down through the fabric ¼ inch (.5 cm) away from where it came up. Pull it tight.

You just made one straight stitch!

FINISHING OFF

Keep your stitches from **unraveling**. When you finish a seam, knot the thread near the fabric. Cut off the extra thread.

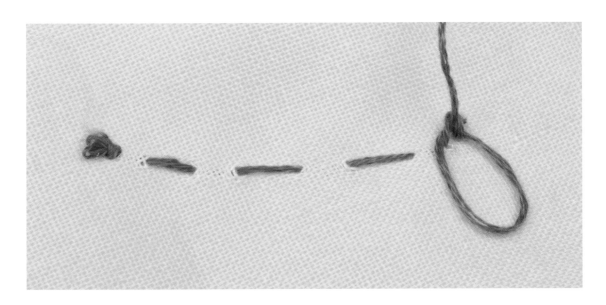

THE RUNNING STITCH (P. 13)

THE BACKSTITCH (P. 14)

THE WHIPSTITCH (P. 15)

STARTING UP

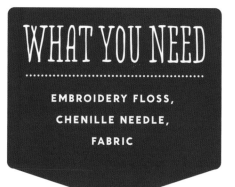

GET GOING WITH
THESE DIRECTIONS!

WHAT YOU NEED

EMBROIDERY FLOSS,
CHENILLE NEEDLE,
FABRIC

THE RUNNING STITCH

 Make one straight stitch.

 Move over ¼ inch (.5 cm). Make another straight stitch.

 Continue making straight stitches ¼ inch (.5 cm) apart.

 Make sewing a running stitch even easier! Push the needle up through the fabric. Keep the needle in front of the fabric. Pinch the fabric. Push the needle through both layers.

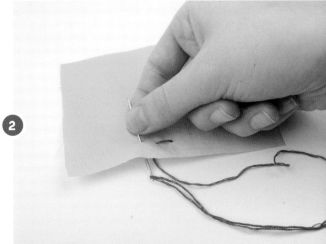

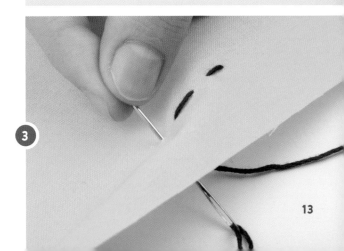

13

THE BACKSTITCH

 Make one straight stitch. Move over ¼ inch (.5 cm). Push the needle up through the fabric to the front.

 Move back to the end of the first stitch. Push the needle down right next to it.

 Continue pushing the needle up through the fabric a stitch ahead. Push it back down at the end of the previous stitch.

THE WHIPSTITCH

 Line up two pieces
of fabric. Push the
needle up through
both layers ¼ inch
(.5 cm) from the edge.

 Move the needle
around the edge of
the fabric. Push the
needle up from the
back again. Pull it
tight.

 Continue making
stitches around the
edge of the fabric. Try
to keep them even.
Only sew up from the
back of the fabric.

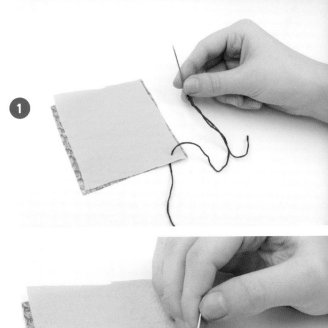

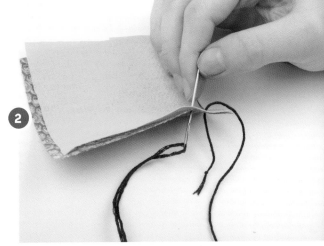

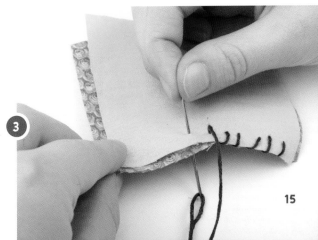

GRAB-AND-GO TOTE

MAKE IT IN NO TIME!

WHAT YOU NEED

FABRIC, EMBROIDERY
FLOSS, RIBBON, SCISSORS,
#18 CHENILLE NEEDLE,
PINS, SAFETY PIN

1 Cut two rectangles of fabric. They should each measure 8 inches (20 cm) by 11 inches (28 cm).

2 Put the fabric rectangles together with the front sides facing in. Lay them down with the short edges on the top and bottom. Put a pin on the right long edge 2 inches (5 cm) from the top.

3 Thread the needle. Straight stitch the left side, the bottom, and the right side up to the pin. Finish off the seam. Take out the pin.

4 Fold the edges of the top down 1 inch (2.5 cm) on each side. Pin the edges in place.

5 Thread the needle. Sew a running stitch along each side ½ inch (1.3 cm) from the folded edge. Take the pins out as you sew. Finish off the seams.

6 Attach a safety pin to one end of the ribbon. Push the pin into the space made by the folded edge. Feed it through one side and then back through the other side. Remove the pin. Turn the bag right side out.

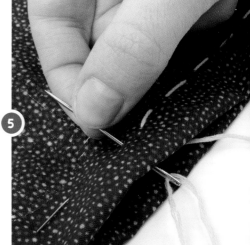

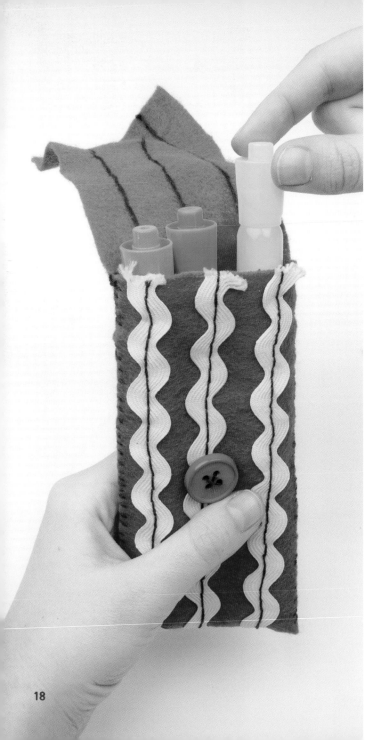

ZIGZAG PENCIL CASE

WHAT YOU NEED

FELT, SCISSORS,
EMBROIDERY FLOSS,
ZIGZAG RIBBON, PINS,
#5 EMBROIDERY NEEDLE,
BUTTON,
MEASURING TAPE

1. Cut a piece of **felt** that is 3 inches (7.5 cm) by 17 inches (43 cm). Lay it flat.

2. Cut three ribbons 17 inches (43 cm) long. Arrange the ribbons on the felt. They should be evenly spaced. Pin the ribbons in place at each end.

3. Thread the needle with three strands of thread. Backstitch down the center of one of the ribbons. Finish off the seam. Take the pins out. Sew other ribbons the same way.

4. Lay the felt flat with the ribbons facing down. Fold up the bottom 6 inches (15 cm). Whipstitch along the left side. Knot in back to finish. Sew the right side the same way.

5. Sew a button onto the front of the pouch. Fold the top flap down. Cut a hole where it covers the button.

CATTY
COIN PURSE

THIS PET WILL EAT
YOUR CHANGE!

WHAT YOU NEED

COTTON FABRIC,
4-INCH (10 CM) ZIPPER,
SCISSORS, GOOGLY
EYES, BUTTON, SEWING
THREAD, #5 EMBROIDERY
NEEDLE, SAFETY PINS

Cut two 5-inch (12.7 cm) circles out of fabric. Cut out four triangles with 3-inch (7.5 cm) sides.

 Put two of the triangles together with the front sides facing in. Whipstitch along two of the edges. Finish off the seams. Turn the triangle right side out. Sew the other two triangles together the same way. These are the ears.

Cut one circle in half. Lay one of the halves down front side up. Lay the zipper face down on top of the half circle. Line the edge of the zipper up with the straight side of the half circle.

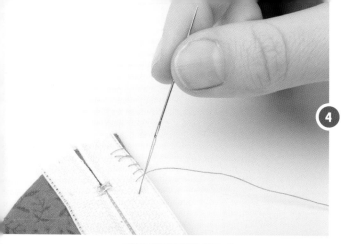

 Thread the needle. Whipstitch the zipper and fabric edges together. Sew close to the zipper. Finish off the seam.

 Lay the second half circle down front side up. Lay the first half circle front side down on top of the second half circle. Line the edge of the zipper up with the straight side of the second half circle. Whipstitch the zipper and fabric edges together. Finish off the seam.

 Sew googly eyes onto one half of the circle. Sew on a button for the nose.

Use a safety pin to attach the open edge of each ear above the eyes. Make the ears hang over the fabric's front side. Unzip the zipper.

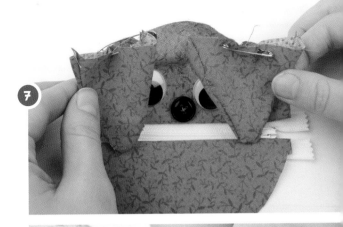

 Lay the circle with the zipper down front side up. Lay the second circle front side down on top of it. Whipstitch around the edge. Be sure to stitch through the pinned ears.

9 Finish off the seam. Take out the safety pins. Turn the purse right side out through the open zipper.

 Try making different animals!

SAVE THE PLANET PILLOW

RECYCLE YOUR FAVORITE TEES!

WHAT YOU NEED

CHALK, #18 CHENILLE
NEEDLE, T-SHIRT,
EMBROIDERY FLOSS,
SCISSORS, MEASURING
TAPE, STUFFING

Use chalk to draw a 10-inch (25 cm) by 8-inch (20 cm) rectangle on shirt.

 Cut out the rectangle through both layers of the shirt.

 Put the rectangles together with the front sides facing in. Whipstitch along three of the edges. Whipstitch the fourth edge but leave a 2-inch (5 cm) opening. Finish off the seam.

 Turn the shirt right side out. Put the stuffing inside.

 Fold the edges of the opening to the inside. Whipstitch the opening closed. Finish off the seam.

 Try stitching squares from more than one shirt together. Make a really big pillow!

25

SONGBIRD
GADGET POUCH

PERFECT FOR HOLDING
YOUR MUSIC!

WHAT YOU NEED

EMBROIDERY FLOSS
(BLUE, BLACK, WHITE,
YELLOW), FELT (RED,
BLUE, BLACK, WHITE AND
YELLOW), #5 EMBROIDERY
NEEDLE, MEASURING
TAPE, SCISSORS, PENCIL

1. 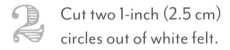 Draw 5½-inch (14 cm) by 4-inch (10 cm) rectangles on red and blue **felt**. Cut both rectangles out.

2. 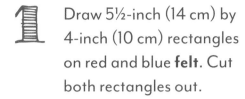 Cut two 1-inch (2.5 cm) circles out of white felt.

3. Cut two ½-inch (1 cm) circles out of black felt.

4. Cut a triangle with 1-inch (2.5 cm) sides out of yellow felt.

5. Cut a 4-inch (10 cm) circle out of blue felt. Cut the blue circle in half.

 Lay a half circle in the corner of the red rectangle. Line the flat edge of the half circle up with a long side of the rectangle.

 Thread the needle with three strands of blue floss. Stitch a running stitch along the curved edge of the circle. Finish off the seam. Sew the other half circle next to the first one the same way.

 Lay the white circles on the red rectangle above the blue half circles.

Put the black circles on top of the white circles. Thread the needle with three strands of black floss. Make one stitch on each circle to keep them in place. Finish off the stitches.

 Put the yellow triangle under the eyes. Thread the needle with three strands of yellow floss. Stitch a running stitch around the edges. Finish off the seam.

 Put the red rectangle on top of the blue rectangle. Thread the needle with three strands of blue floss. Whipstitch along the sides and bottom. Finish off the seam.

Keep Sewing!

You can sew almost anything! You can make cool stuff for yourself. Or make gifts for family and friends. There are tons of things to sew.

Explore craft and fabric stores. Check out books on sewing at the library. Look up sewing tips and projects online. Get inspired and create your own designs. Use sewing to mend your clothes. Or to make them into something new. Use sewing to make art. It's all about using your creativity!

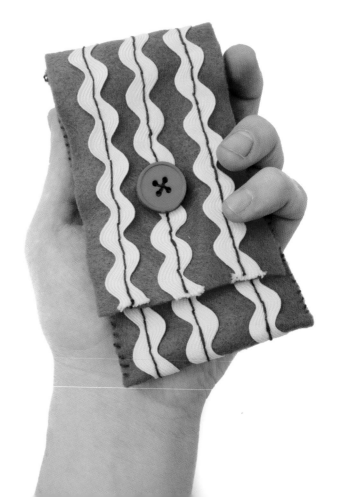

GLOSSARY

CHENILLE – a type of thick, fuzzy fabric.

COMPLICATED – having many parts, details, ideas, or functions.

FELT – a soft, thick fabric.

OVERVIEW – the general idea or summary of something.

PATTERN – a sample or guide used to make something.

TAPESTRY – a heavy, woven wall hanging with pictures or designs on it.

UNRAVEL – to come apart or to come undone.

WEB SITES

To learn more about fiber art, visit ABDO online at www.abdopublishing.com. Web sites about creative ways for kids to make fiber art are featured on our Book Links page. These links are routinely monitored and updated to provide the most current information available.

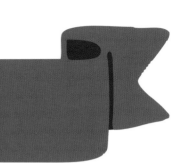

INDEX

DATE DUE

			PRINTED IN U.S.A